PENGUIN CLASSICS

FRAGMENTS

Besides seven books of original poetry, BROOKS HAXTON has published two other translations, *Selected Poems* by Victor Hugo and *Dances for Flute and Thunder*, an anthology of poems from the ancient Greek nominated for the PEN translation award. He is the recipient of many honors and awards including fellowships from the Guggenheim Foundation and the National Endowment for the Arts.

JAMES HILLMAN has written more than twenty books, including *The Dream and the Underworld*, *The Force of Character*, *Reinventing Psychiatry* (nominated for a Pulitzer Prize in 1975), and *The Soul's Code*, which debuted in 1996 on the *New York Times* Bestseller list at # 1. He is an internationally renowned lecturer, teacher, and psychologist who has taught at Yale, Syracuse, the University of Chicago, and the University of Dallas. Hillman graduated from Trinity College, Dublin, and was the director of the Jung Institute in Zurich.

[handwritten note:] mutual succession is an act of amity.

HERACLITUS

Fragments

Translated by BROOKS HAXTON
With a Foreword by JAMES HILLMAN

PENGUIN BOOKS

PENGUIN BOOKS

Published by the Penguin Group
Penguin Group (USA) Inc., 375 Hudson Street, New York, New York 10014, U.S.A.
Penguin Books Ltd, 80 Strand, London WC2R 0RL, England
Penguin Books Australia Ltd, 250 Camberwell Road,
Camberwell, Victoria 3124, Australia
Penguin Books Canada Ltd, 10 Alcorn Avenue, Toronto, Ontario, Canada M4V 3B2
Penguin Books India (P) Ltd, 11 Community Centre,
Panchsheel Park, New Delhi – 110 017, India
Penguin Books (N.Z.) Ltd, Cnr Rosedale and Airborne Roads,
Albany, Auckland, New Zealand
Penguin Books (South Africa) (Pty) Ltd, 24 Sturdee Avenue,
Rosebank, Johannesburg 2196, South Africa

Penguin Books Ltd, Registered Offices: 80 Strand, London WC2R 0RL, England

First published in the United States of America by Viking Penguin,
a member of Penguin Putnam Inc. 2001
Published in Penguin Books 2003

3   5   7   9   10   8   6   4   2

Translation copyright © Brooks Haxton, 2001
Foreword copyright © James Hillman, 2001
All rights reserved

THE LIBRARY OF CONGRESS HAS CATALOGED THE HARDCOVER EDITION AS FOLLOWS:
Heraclitus, of Ephesus.
[Fragments, English & Greek]
Fragments : the collected wisdom of Heraclitus / translated by
Brooks Haxton ; with a foreword by James Hillman.
p.   cm.
ISBN 0-670-89195-9 (hc.)
ISBN 0 14 24.3765 4 (pbk.)
1. Philosophy, Ancient.   I. Haxton, Brooks, 1950–   II. Title.
B220.E5 H39 2001
182'.4—dc21   00-043368

Printed in the United States of America
Set in Baskerville Greek Polytonic and Giovanni Book
Designed by Francesca Belanger

for Mary Karr

Acknowledgments

The translator would like to thank everyone at Viking who helped to see this book through publication, especially the editor, Michael Millman, for his friendly intelligence, Zelimir Galjanic for thoughtful attention to detail, and Susan Petersen Kennedy for her guiding interest and enthusiasm. Thanks also to my good friend, Ken Frieden, who read an early draft of the translation and offered helpful suggestions and encouragement.

Contents

Foreword: "I am as I am not"

Because archetypal modes of thought transcend
time and place, the insights of Heraclitus are strik-
ingly postmodern. Although conceived five hun-
dred years before our era in the Greek city of
Ephesus, his poetic aphorisms show a deconstruc-
tive mind at work. The life of thought does not
necessarily progress, for, as he says, "Any day
stands equal to the rest" (120). Since moving for-
ward and moving back are one and the same (69),
the latest postmodern thinking completes the cir-
cle where Heraclitus began: "The beginning is the
end" (70).

Early Greek thinkers sought the stuff of which
the world was made. For Thales, it was water; for
Anaximenes, air; for Anaximander, a combination
of hot and cold. Empedocles expanded the stuff
to four indestructible elemental principles, while
Anaxagoras is said to have proposed innumerable
generative seeds composing the nature of things.
The Atomists abstracted the seeds yet further, pro-

posing multiple particles moving in a void. The Pythagoreans found the truth of the world lies in numbers, their proportions and relations, and Parmenides, the most metaphysical of them all, laid out his theory of the cosmos through the sheer power of logical thought.

Heraclitus took a different tack. His method is more psychological. He posited no basic substance, nor did he abstract the world of the senses into numbers, atoms, or assertions about Being as a whole. Instead he said, nothing is stable; all is in flux. Whatever you say about anything, its opposite is equally true. He brought language into the game of cosmological thinking. Declarations will always be self-contradictory, relative, subjective. "People dull their wits with gibberish, and cannot use their ears and eyes" (4). "They lack the skill to listen or to speak" (6). You cannot know the world in the manner of natural philosophy or mathematics or deductive logic. Because: "By cosmic rule . . . all things change" (36). "The sun is new again, all day" (32). "The river where you set your foot just now is gone—those waters giving way to this, now this" (41).

His name for this changing flux, or process, in today's terms, is "fire," a metaphor for the shifting meanings of all truth. Therefore, the verbal account, or *logos*, of the world is also fire. Truth, wisdom, knowledge, reality—none can stand apart from this fire that allows no objective fixity.

Heraclitean fire, it must be insisted, is neither a metaphysical essence like the elements of his peers, nor a spiritual energy, nor a material substance, the fire that burns your hand. His fire is metaphorical, a psychological intensity that penetrates through all literalisms, a quicksilver fire that flows through the hand, burning away whatever tries to grasp reality and hold it firm. This fire, as the active principle of deconstruction, brilliantly deconstructs itself.

You can, however, reflect your own mind, see into your own thoughts. You can become psychological or, as he puts it, "Applicants for wisdom do what I have done: inquire within" (80). "People ought to know themselves" (106). This psychological turn means you cannot know the psyche no matter how endless your search (71), since consciousness is always also its opposite, unconsciousness. How better say this than: "I am as I am not" (81).

Statements pertaining to sleep add support to my notion of Heraclitus the psychologist. Rather than a focus upon the healing efficacy of dreams as in the Asclepian cult of his time or upon their prognostic meaning as summed up in Egyptian and later Greek writing by Artemidorus, Heraclitus simply states that the *logos* is active in sleep. Even while you are resting, the fire burns. Dreaming is the flickering activity of the mind participating in the world's imagination. Whether the dream helps us feel better and sleep better, cures our distress, or prefigures our destiny, is less its essential nature than its energetic spontaneity. During sleep, we may be each apart from the commonly shared day-world, yet the never-resting *logos* goes on producing images ever new as the sun each day, as the river's flowing. In our private rest, the restlessness of the cosmos continues to do its work.

For all the puzzling juxtapositions—hot/cold, pure/tainted, war/peace, plenty/famine—that quicken the reader's speculations, Heraclitus insists on a keen practical sense of things. No lofty idealism or dulling generalities that smooth over life's honest hardness. "Hungry livestock, though in sight of pasture, need the prod" (55). "War makes us as we are" (62). "The poet was a fool who wanted no conflict" (43). "The mind . . . needs strength" (45).

No sloppy emotionalism either. Heraclitus would hardly be found among enthusiastic revivalists or holistic healers of the New Age. "Dry, the soul grows wise and good" (74). "Moisture makes the soul succumb . . ." (72), which I have understood to be a warning against drowning in easiness. Comfortable, complacent, content— these soporifics extinguish the fire of the soul.

Moreover, no religiosity. Fragments 116 onward state pithy truths that do not let us escape into wishful denials of realities. "Those who mouth high talk may think themselves high-minded" (118). Neither your hope nor your fantasies tell you anything about what comes after death (122). The unknown is not revealed by faith (116). Fate is not governed from elsewhere, but is in your character, the way you bear yourself each day (121). Because humans understand so little of the gods (126), the initiations and mysteries we practice are not true holiness (125).

Haxton's English captures Heraclitus's tough-mindedness: "One thunderbolt strikes root through everything" (28). "War, as father of all things, and king . . . (44). "Hunger, even in the elements, and insolence" (24). "The mind . . . that strains against itself, needs strength, as does the arm . . ." (45).

The Heraclitean vision is Greek: the inhuman nature of the gods is borne out by the facts of nature and by the tragic flaws in human biography. The fire is demanding, and it takes its toll.

As well as giving a vision of the nature of things and the truth of the world we live in, the passages state a poetics of dissonance—another reason Heraclitus has appeal for writers, artists, and psychologists. In the heart of the mind there is a tension. We are pulled apart, enflamed, and at risk. Therefore, our expressions must hold the tension so as to bespeak accurately and poignantly the actual soul as it exists. "How, from a fire that never sinks or sets, would you escape?" (27).

Heraclitus has also bequeathed to Western culture a mode of expressing this fire: the aphoristic phrase. The body of work attributed to him consists in a collection of incendiary sparks that scholarship calls "fragments," as if to say the work is incomplete, only shards of a lost whole. But scholarship misses the fact that the style is the message. The snapshot, the *aperçu*, reveals things as they are: "The eye, the ear, the mind in action, these I value" (13). To speculate about the lost book distracts from the power of the fragments and their message: all things change, all things flow. The world is revealed only in quick glances. There can be no completion. "Things keep their secrets" (10), because they cannot be fixed into the comprehensive formulations of a book. No sooner known and explained, the event has changed. Therefore, "the known way is an impasse" (7).

Faced with this impasse, usual thinkers try to grasp the flow either by religious mystification or by overprecise and reductive explanations (11). Whereas the thinker (the "true prophet") who is on track speaks in signs, much like gestures, hints, and metaphors that neither reveal nor conceal. These signs allow for many meanings with ambiguous and suggestive possibilities. Again, I see a parallel with the psychological approach to interpretation. It favors responses in metaphors, images, sharp-pointed insights that stir the mind to awakened observation and deepened reflection.

We are still riddling out these "fragments" generation after generation in ever-new, and necessary, fresh translations. Translations age, even though the original texts do not. In fact, classic texts are rejuvenated by virtue of fresh translation. If all things flow, then each translation must be different from every other one, yet still be the same, much as Heraclitus's river. Or, to say it otherwise, the sun is new every day—and Haxton offers a translation for this day, our day.

Heraclitus has moved philosophers from Plato

through Nietzsche, Whitehead, Heidegger, and Jung, and as Haxton says in his admirably condensed introduction, it is mainly from philosophers (ancient writers and Church Fathers) that the fragments have been culled and passed on. Therefore, everything we read and refer to as "Heraclitus" is second- or thirdhand—even fourth, in that the Greek and Latin have been turned into English. What Heraclitus actually said, or wrote, we have only signs pointing to the authority of a half-revealed, half-concealed author. I like to think he would have enjoyed this deconstruction of his lasting words through the centuries of time.

James Hillman

Introduction

When the iron hoe was a new invention, Pythagoras saw mathematical logic as a language of cosmic prophecy. Now, when we say $E = mc^2$, we are stating in mathematical terms the thought of Pythagoras's contemporary, Heraclitus, who said that energy is the essence of matter. Heraclitus put it in the ancient Greek this way:

> All things change to fire,
> and fire exhausted
> falls back into things.

Einstein agreed. For him, the earth, the sun and moon and stars, the winds and waters, everything, became energy in flux, in relativity, and the world was staggered by mental shock, then by physical explosions. But the wisdom of Heraclitus held true twenty-five hundred years after his death.

Heir to the throne in Ephesus, one of the world's richest and most powerful cities, Heraclitus gave up the kingdom and chose, instead of the trappings of power, to seek the Word of wisdom. His writings survived the Persian empire, dominant in his time, and then the Greek, and Roman. For hundreds of years, great writers, Plato, Aristotle, Marcus Aurelius, and others, quoted him with respect. Then, his book, with thousands of the finest works of that world, disappeared forever.

Scholars describe this lost book as the first coherent philosophical treatise. But the existing fragments resemble prophecy and poetry as much as they do philosophical discourse. After all, philosophy had just begun. Pythagoras had only lately coined the word "philosopher," meaning lover of wisdom. But the pursuit of wisdom is much older than Pythagoras or his word for himself as a serious student.

Heraclitus uses the word for wisdom, *sophos*, thirteen times in the surviving fragments of his work. The one time he mentions philosophers, he speaks of their need for learning. But he says that wisdom is beyond learning and beyond cleverness: "Of all the words yet spoken none comes quite as far as wisdom, which is the action of the mind beyond all things that may be said." "Wisdom," he says, "is the oneness of mind that guides and permeates all things." For Heraclitus, wisdom, much like fire, is the very essence of the cosmos.

Before Heraclitus, the traditions most attentive to this oneness existed in various cultures as wisdom poetry. Farther to the east, Gautama Buddha, another prince who deserted his kingdom for the pursuit of wisdom, was an exact contemporary of Heraclitus, as were the legendary Lao-tzu and Confucius, all closely associated with poetic traditions of wisdom.

Wisdom poetry is often allied with religion, but it is distinct from the religious poetries of prayer, praise, and narrative, because it focuses above all on the task of speaking wisdom. The wisdom books best known in European cultures are Proverbs, Ecclesiastes, and Job. Anyone can see marked similarities between the so-called pessimism of Heraclitus and that in the Book of Ecclesiastes, written not far to the south during the same century.

Equally striking similarities may be found between the wisdom of Heraclitus and that in other traditions. A man disillusioned to the point of wanting to die, in the famous Egyptian *Dispute Between a Man and His Soul*, for example, feels trapped, like those said by Heraclitus to be "confined in the sodden lumber of the body." The

Egyptian seeks "the movement of eternal return."
He awaits "the Mystical Encounter with the Lord
of Transformations hidden in [his] body," this
Lord being the falcon god Sokar, who disappears
with his prey into the fire of the sun.*

All this represents the body, fire, death, and
transformation much as Heraclitus would de-
scribe them more than a thousand years later.
Heraclitus says of the dead: "Corpses, like night
soil, get carted off . . ."; "Souls change into water
on their way toward death . . ."; and "Fire of all
things is the judge and ravisher." The Egyptian
poet says of the dead man "cast from his house
and flung upon the hill" that "the flood takes
him, the sun takes him, fish talk to him in shallow
water."

Most germane to Heraclitus of all these tradi-
tions may be the Persian. Persia in his time, con-
solidated under Darius to control almost all of Asia
Minor, was the inheritor of the legacy of Sumer,
with a two-thousand-year-old tradition of wis-
dom poetry. Persia's most powerful new religion
was the worship of the Lord Wisdom, Ahura
Mazda, as taught by the prophet Zarathustra, who

*See Bika Reed's *Rebel in the Soul: An Ancient Egyptian Dia-
logue Between a Man and His Destiny* (Rochester, Vt.: Inner
Traditions International, 1997).

lived earlier in the same century as Heraclitus. A tenet of Zoroastrian teaching was the identification of wisdom with an ever-living fire, *pyr aeizôon*, as Heraclitus calls his version.

Such resemblances are too poignant to ignore, and who would want to ignore them, and why? But historical connections are doubtful. Heraclitus never mentions the Lord Wisdom. Yet the word *theos* does appear nine times among the fragments. Scholars differ in their exact sense of the tone and meaning of this word, which is translated most literally as "god." Clearly, Heraclitus meant to distinguish his attitude from others more prevalent at the time. He says:

> They raise their voices
> at stone idols
> as a man might argue
> with his doorpost,
> they have understood
> so little of the gods.

The conventional presences of the Greek gods hover at the edges of these fragments, especially Apollo, god of prophecy and cosmic fire, but *theos* also refers to a presence distinct from any mythological person. This presence is as vital to the thought of Heraclitus as are wisdom, the Word, and fire. Heraclitus makes this clear when he speaks of the rule of *theos* in fragment 36:

> By cosmic rule,
> as day yields night,
> so winter summer,
> war peace, plenty famine.
> All things change.
> Fire penetrates the lump
> of myrrh, until the joining
> bodies die and rise again
> in smoke called incense.

In another of the fragments, Heraclitus hints at his kinship with the poets and prophets, when he says, "Without obscurity or needless explanation the true prophet signifies." The very closeness of this association may account for the need in Heraclitus to set his work apart, when he says outright, "We need no longer take the poets and myth-makers for sure witnesses about disputed facts."

Heraclitus is at equal pains to distinguish himself from philosophers he mentions, and from his contemporaries in general, from the few who consider wisdom, without understanding, and from the many who make no attempt.

To a sober mind, the drunkenness of cultic worshippers must have been particularly unappealing in a cosmopolitan city like Ephesus, with gods of wine on every side, drunken Greeks initiated into the Thracian ecstasies of Dionysus running amok with drunken Phrygians worshiping Sabazius, Lydians possessed by Bassareus, and Cretans in the frenzy of Zagreus, all claiming in their cups to have transcended understanding.

Despite good reasons to distrust the thinking of others, and to disapprove their actions, Heraclitus argues movingly for truths that any thinking person can understand:

> Since mindfulness, of all things,
> is the ground of being,
> to speak one's true mind,
> and to keep things known
> in common, serves all being,
> just as laws made clear
> uphold the city . . .

At this task of speaking his true mind, ancient and modern readers agree, Heraclitus is among the greatest writers of his language, comparable for the shapeliness and power of his style even to the finest writer of his lifetime, the first of the great playwrights, Aeschylus. This liveliness of style is all the more engaging because the life of Heraclitus is also remarkable. An early and abiding influence on Christian thought is famously transparent in the Heraclitean language that opens the Gospel According to John: "In the beginning was the Word, and the Word was with God, and the Word was God." The scientific purport of Heraclitus has remained startling and valuable for twenty-five hundred years, his social satire has kept its edge, and his contributions to philosophy, formative in his time, have been enduring.

Ironically, the great writer keeps insisting upon the limits of his art as a way toward wisdom. He says, "To a god the wisdom of the wisest man sounds apish. Beauty in a human face looks apish too. In everything we have attained the excellence of apes."

This is funny, first of all, and very dark as its persuasiveness sinks in, but finally it reveals itself to be the lucid darkness of a truth that speakers of English at the present millennium are still privileged to consider. "To be evenminded is the greatest virtue," Heraclitus still persuades us. "Wisdom is to speak the truth and act in keeping with its nature."

A Note on the Translation

Naturally, I had read translations of Heraclitus in English before I did my own. The first was the excellent version Philip Wheelwright did in the 1950s. Later, Guy Davenport published another fine translation in the 1970s. As I worked, I referred to several versions, most closely to the Loeb Classical Library text, edited and translated by H. W. S. Jones, whose literal translation guided me through the Greek. Jones in his work followed the nineteenth-century text assembled by Ingram Bywater, using the subsequent scholarship of Jacob Bernays, Hermann Diels, and others. Scholarship on Heraclitus that has shaped my thinking includes work by Charles Burnet, G. S. Kirk, and Charles H. Kahn.

The existing fragments of Heraclitus are divided into three types: supposedly direct quotations, reputed paraphrases, and commentaries. Since the accuracy of these sources can never be established, I have tried to make the most of what we have by tailoring paraphrase and commentary to fit stylistically with quotes. I chose this procedure for the sake of a reader's sustained connection with my English version, confident that those misled by my approach can easily turn to the excellent scholarship available. My translation uses free verse to suggest the poetic ring of the original prose, which deserves to be called poetry as much as the metrical writings of thinkers like Empedocles and Parmenides.

Aside from this general procedure, I have stayed close to literal paraphrase, wherever this seemed adequate, and where I have deviated, I have tried to explain my thinking in the notes at the end of this volume.

FRAGMENTS

1

Τοῦ δὲ λόγου τοῦδ' ἐόντος αἰεὶ ἀξύνετοι
γίνονται ἄνφρωποι καὶ πρόσθεν ἢ ἀκοῦσαι καὶ
ἀκούσαντες τὸ πρῶτον. γινομένων γὰρ πάντων
κατὰ τὸν λόγον τόνδε ἀπείροισι ἐοίκασι
πειρώμενοι καὶ ἐπέων καὶ ἔργων τοιουτέων
ὁκοίων ἐγὼ διηγεῦμαι, διαιρέων ἕκαστον κατὰ
φύσιν καὶ φράζων ὅκως ἔχει. τοὺς δὲ ἄλλους
ἀνθρώπους λανθάνει ὁκόσα ἐγερθέντες
ποιέουσι, ὅκωσπερ ὁκόσα εὕδοντες
ἐπιλανθάνονται.

1

The Word proves
those first hearing it
as numb to understanding
as the ones who have not heard.

Yet all things follow from the Word.

Some, blundering
with what I set before you,
try in vain with empty talk
to separate the essences of things
and say how each thing truly is.

And all the rest make no attempt.
They no more see
how they behave broad waking
than remember clearly
what they did asleep.

2

Οὐκ ἐμεῦ ἀλλὰ τοῦ λόγου ἀκούσαντας
ὁμολογέειν σοφόν ἐστι, ἓν πάντα εἶναι.

3

Ἀξύνετοι ἀκούσαντες κωφοῖσι ἐοίκασι· φάτις
αὐτοῖσι μαρτυρέει παρεόντας ἀπεῖναι.

4

Κακοὶ μάρτυρες ἀνθρώποισι ὀφθαλμοὶ καὶ
ὦτα, βαρβάρους ψυχὰς ἐχόντων.

5

Οὐ φρονέουσι τοιαῦτα πολλοὶ ὀκόσοισι
ἐγκυρέουσι οὐδὲ μαθόντες γινώσκουσι,
ἑωυτοῖσι δὲ δοκέουσι.

2

For wisdom, listen
not to me but to the Word,
and know that all is one.

3

Those unmindful when they hear,
for all they make of their intelligence,
may be regarded as the walking dead.

4

People dull their wits with gibberish,
and cannot use their ears and eyes.

5

Many fail to grasp what they have seen,
and cannot judge what they have learned,
although they tell themselves they know.

6

Ἀκοῦσαι οὐκ ἐπιστάμενοι οὐδ' εἰπεῖν.

7

Ἐὰν μὴ ἔλπηαι, ἀνέλπιστον οὐκ ἐξευρήσει,
ἀνεξερεύνητον ἐὸν καὶ ἄπορον.

8

Χρυσὸν οἱ διζήμενοι γῆν πολλὴν ὀρύσσουσι
καὶ εὑρίσκουσι ὀλίγον.

9

Ἀγχιβασίην.

6

Yet they lack the skill
to listen or to speak.

7

Whoever cannot seek
the unforeseen sees nothing,
for the known way
is an impasse.

8

Men dig tons of earth
to find an ounce of gold.

9

See note.

10

Φύσις κρύπτεσθαι φιλεῖ.

11

Ὁ ἄναξ οὗ τὸ μαντεῖόν ἐστι τὸ ἐν Δελφοῖς,
οὔτε λέγει οὔτε κρύπτει, ἀλλά σημαίνει.

12

Σίβυλλα δὲ μαινομένῳ στόματι ἀγέλαστα καὶ
ἀκαλλώπιστα καὶ ἀμύριστα φθεγγομένη χιλίων
ἐτέων ἐξικνέεται τῇ φωνῇ διὰ τὸν θεόν.

13

Ὅσων ὄψις ἀκοὴ μάθησις, ταῦτα ἐγὼ
προτιμέω.

10

✳ Things keep their secrets.

11

Yet without obscurity
or needless explanation
the true prophet signifies.

12

The prophet's voice possessed of god
requires no ornament, no sweetening of tone,
but carries over a thousand years.

Define "god"

13

The eye, the ear,
the mind in action,
these I value.

14

Τοῦτο γὰρ ἴδιόν ἐστι τῶν νῦν καιρῶν, ἐν οἷς
πάντων πλωτῶν καὶ πορευτῶν γεγονότων οὐκ
ἂν ἔτι πρέπον εἴ ποιηταῖς καὶ μυθογράφοις
χρῆσθαι μάρτυσι περὶ τῶν ἀγνοουμένων, ὅπερ
οἱ πρὸ ἡμῶν περὶ τῶν πλείστων, ἀπίστους
ἀμφισβητουμένων παρεχόμενοι βεβαιωτὰς
κατὰ τὸν Ἡράκλειτον.

15

Ὀφθαλμοὶ τῶν ὤτων ἀκριβέστεροι μάρτυρες.

16

Πολυμαθίν νόον ἔχειν οὐ διδάσκει·
Ἡσίοδον γὰρ ἂν ἐδίδαξε καὶ Πυθαγόρην·
αὖτίς τε Ξενοφάνεα καὶ Ἑκαταῖον.

14

Now that we can travel anywhere,
we need no longer take the poets
and myth-makers for sure witnesses
about disputed facts.

15

What eyes witness,
ears believe on hearsay.

16

If learning were a path of wisdom,
those most learned about myth
would not believe, with Hesiod,
that Pallas in her wisdom gloats
over the noise of battle.

17

Πυθαγόρης Μνησάρχου ἱστορίην ἤσκησε
ἀνθρώπων μάλιστα πάντων. καὶ ἐκλεξάμενος
ταύτας τὰς συγγραφὰς ἐποιήσατο ἑωυτοῦ
σοφίην, πολυμαθίην, κακοτεχνίην.

18

Ὁκόσων λόγους ἤκουσα οὐδεὶς ἀφικνέεται ἐς
τοῦτο, ὥστε γινώσκειν ὅτι σοφόν ἐστι πάντων
κεχωρισμένον.

19

Ἕν τὸ σοφόν, ἐπίστασθαι γνώμην ᾗ
κυβερνᾶται πάντα διὰ πάντων.

17

Pythagoras may well have been
the deepest in his learning of all men.
And still he claimed to recollect
details of former lives,
being in one a cucumber
and one time a sardine.

18

Of all the words yet spoken,
none comes quite as far as wisdom,
which is the action of the mind
beyond all things that may be said.

19

Wisdom is the oneness
of mind that guides
and permeates all things.

20

Κόσμον τόνδε τὸν αὐτὸν ἁπάντων οὔτε τις
θεῶν οὔτε ἀνθρώπων ἐποίησε, ἀλλ' ἦν αἰεὶ καὶ
ἔστι καὶ ἔσται πῦρ ἀείζωον ἁπτόμενον μέτρα
καὶ ἀποσβεννύμενον μέτρα.

21

Πυρὸς τροπαὶ πρῶτον θάλασσα· θαλάσσης δὲ
τὸ μὲν ἥμισυ γῆ, τὸ δὲ ἥμισυ πρηστήρ.

22

Πυρὸς ἀνταμείβεται πάντα καὶ πῦρ ἁπάντων,
ὥσπερ χρυσοῦ χρήματα καὶ χρημάτων χρυσός.

20

That which always was,
and is, and will be everliving fire,
the same for all, the cosmos,
made neither by god nor man,
replenishes in measure
as it burns away.

21

Fire in its ways of changing
is a sea transfigured
between forks of lightning
and the solid earth.

22

As all things change to fire,
and fire exhausted
falls back into things,
the crops are sold
for money spent on food.

23

Θάλασσα διαχέεται καὶ μετρέεται ἐς τὸν αὐτὸν
λόγον ὁκοῖος πρόσθεν ἦν ἢ γενέσθαι.

24

Χρησμοσύνη . . . κόρος.

25

Ζῇ πῦρ τὸν ἀέρος θάνατον, καὶ ἀὴρ ζῇ τὸν
πυρὸς θάνατον· ὕδωρ ζῇ τὸν γῆς θάνατον, γῆ
τὸν ὕδατος.

23

The earth is melted
into the sea
by that same reckoning
whereby the sea
sinks into the earth.

24

Hunger, even
in the elements,
and insolence.

25

Air dies giving birth
to fire. Fire dies
giving birth to air. Water,
thus, is born of dying
earth, and earth of water.

26

Πάντα τὸ πῦρ ἐπελθὸν κρινέει καὶ
καταλήψεται.

27

Τὸ μὴ δῦνόν ποτε πῶς ἄν τις λάθοι ;

28

Τὰ δὲ πάντα οἰακίζει κεραυνός.

29

Ἥλιος οὐχ ὑπερβήσεται μέτρα· εἰ δὲ μή,
Ἐρινύες μιν δίκης ἐπίκουροι εξευρήσουσι.

26

Fire of all things
is the judge and ravisher.

27

How, from a fire
that never sinks
or sets,
would you escape?

28

One thunderbolt strikes
root through everything.

29

No being, not the sun
itself, exceeds due measure,
but contending powers
set things right.

30

Ἠοῦς καὶ ἑσπέρης τέρματα ἡ ἄρκτος, καὶ
ἀντίον τῆς ἄρκτου οὖρος αἰθρίου Διός.

31

Εἰ μὴ ἥλιος ἦν, ἕνεκα τῶν ἄλλων ἄστρων
εὐφρόνη ἂν ἦν.

32

Νέος ἐφ' ἡμέρῃ ἥλιος.

30

Dawn turns to dusk
around the pivot
of the North.
Southward lies
the zone
of greater light.

31

Without the sun,
what day? What night?

32

The sun is new
again, all day.

33

Δοκεῖ δὲ [Θαλῆς] κατά τινας πρῶτος
ἀστρολογῆσαι καὶ ἡλιακὰς ἐκλείψεις καὶ
τροπὰς προειπεῖν, ὥς φησιν Εὔδημος ἐν τῇ
περὶ τῶν ἀστρολογουμένων ἱστορίᾳ· ὅθεν
αὐτὸν καὶ Ξενοφάνης καὶ Ἡρόδοτος θαυμάζει·
μαρτυρεῖ δ' αὐτῷ καὶ Ἡράκλειτος καὶ
Δημόκριτος.

34

Ὧν ὁ ἥλιος ἐπιστάτης ὢν καὶ σκοπός, ὁρίζειν
καὶ βραβεύειν καὶ ἀναδεικνύναι καὶ
ἀναφαίνειν μεταβολὰς καὶ ὥρας αἳ πάντα
φέρουσι . . .

35

Διδάσκαλος δὲ πλείστων Ἡσίοδος· τοῦτον
ἐπίστανται πλεῖστα εἰδέναι, ὅστις ἡμέρην καὶ
εὐφρόνην οὐκ ἐγίνωσκε· ἔστι γὰρ ἕν.

33

The mind of Thales
saw in forethought—
clearly as in heaven—
the eclipse.

34

The sun, timekeeper
of the day and season,
oversees all things.

35

Many who have learned
from Hesiod the countless names
of gods and monsters
never understand
that night and day are one.

36

Ὁ θεὸς ἡμέρη εὐφρόνη, χειμῶν θέρος,
πόλεμος εἰρήνη, κόρος λιμός· ἀλλοιοῦται δὲ
ὅκωσπερ πῦρ, ὁκόταν συμμιγῇ θυώμασι,
ὀνομάζεται καθ' ἡδονὴν ἑκάστου.

37

Εἰ πάντα τὰ ὄντα καπνὸς γένοιτο, ῥῖνες
ἂν διαγνοῖεν.

38

Αἱ ψυχαὶ ὀσμῶνται καθ' ἅδην.

36

By cosmic rule,
as day yields night,
so winter summer,
war peace, plenty famine.
All things change.
Fire penetrates the lump
of myrrh, until the joining
bodies die and rise again
in smoke called incense.

37

If everything
were turned to smoke,
the nose would
be the seat of judgment.

38

Thus in the abysmal dark
the soul is known by scent.

39

Τὰ ψυχρὰ θέρεται, θέρμον ψύχεται, ὑγρὸν
αὐαίνεται, καρφαλέον νοτίζεται.

40

Σκίδνησι καὶ συνάγει, πρόσεισι καὶ
ἄπεισι.

41

Ποταμοῖσι δὶς τοῖσι αὐτοῖσι οὐκ ἂν
ἐμβαίης· ἕτερα γὰρ <καὶ ἕτερα> ἐπιρρέει
ὕδατα.

39

What was cold soon warms,
and warmth soon cools.
So moisture dries,
and dry things drown.

B126
Continuum

40

What was scattered
gathers.
What was gathered
blows apart.

41

The river
where you set
your foot just now
is gone—
those waters
giving way to this,
now this.

42

Omitted, see note.

43

Καὶ Ἡράκλειτος ἐπιτιμᾷ τῷ ποιήσαντι· ὡς
ἔρις ἔκ τε θεῶν καὶ ἀνθρώπων ἀπόλοιτο· οὐ
γὰρ ἂν εἶναι ἁρμονίαν μὴ ὄντος ὀξέος καὶ
βαρέος, οὐδὲ τὰ ζῷα ἄνευ θήλεος καὶ ἄρρενος,
ἐναντίων ὄντων.

44

Πόλεμος πάντων μὲν πατήρ ἐστι πάντων
δὲ βασιλεύς, καὶ τοὺς μὲν θεοὺς ἔδειξε
τοὺς δὲ ἀνθρώπους, τοὺς μὲν δούλους ἐποίησε
τοὺς δὲ ἐλευθέρους.

43

The poet was a fool
who wanted no conflict
among us, gods
or people.
Harmony needs
low and high,
as progeny needs
man and woman.

44

War, as father
of all things, and king,
names few
to serve as gods,
and of the rest makes
these men slaves,
those free.

45

Οὐ ξυνίασι ὅκως διαφερόμενον ἑωυτῷ
ὁμολογέει· παλίντονος ἁρμονίη ὅκωσπερ τόξου
καὶ λύρης.

46

Καὶ περὶ αὐτῶν τούτων ἀνώτερον
ἐπιζητοῦσι καὶ φυσικώτερον . . . καὶ
Ἡράκλειτος τὸ ἀντίξουν συμφέρον, καὶ ἐκ τῶν
διαφερόντων καλλίστην ἁρμονίαν, καὶ πάντα
κατ᾽ ἔριν γίνεσθαι.

47

Ἁρμονίη ἀφανὴς φανερῆς κρείσσων.

48

Μὴ εἰκῆ περὶ τῶν μεγίστων συμβαλώμεθα.

45

The mind, to think of the accord
that strains against itself,
needs strength, as does the arm
to string the bow or lyre.

46

From the strain
of binding opposites
comes harmony.

47

The harmony past knowing sounds
more deeply than the known.

48

Yet let's not make
rash guesses
our most lucid thoughts.

49

Χρὴ εὖ μάλα πολλῶν ἵστορας φιλοσόφους
ἄνδρας εἶναι.

50

Γναφέων ὁδὸς εὐθεῖα καὶ σκολιὴ μία ἐστὶ
καὶ ἡ αὐτή.

51

Ὄνοι σύρματ᾽ ἂν ἕλοιντο μᾶλλον ἢ
χρυσόν.

49

Seekers of wisdom first
need sound intelligence.

50

Under the comb
the tangle and the straight path
are the same.

51

An ass prefers a bed of litter
to a golden throne.

52

Θάλασσα ὕδωρ καθαρώτατον καὶ
μιαρώτατον, ἰχθύσι μὲν πότιμον καὶ σωτήριον,
ἀνθρώποις δὲ ἄποτον καὶ ὀλέθριον.

53

Sues coeno, cohortales aves pulvere (vel
cinere) lavari.

54

Omitted as repetition of 53.

55

Πᾶν ἑρπετὸν πληγῇ νέμεται.

52

[handwritten: B61]

[handwritten: Fish can live in salt water; man cannot.]

The sea is both pure
and tainted, healthy
and good haven to the fish,
to men impotable and deadly.

53

Poultry bathe
in dust and ashes,
swine in filth.

55

Hungry livestock,
though in sight of pasture,
need the prod.

56

Backward-turning
— stretching
— adjustment

Παλίντονος ἁρμονίη κόσμου ὅκωσπερ
λύρης καὶ τόξου.

57

Ἀγαθὸν καὶ κακὸν ταὐτόν.

58

Καὶ ἀγαθὸν καὶ κακόν [ἕν ἐστι]· οἱ γοῦν
ἰατροί, φησὶν ὁ Ἡράκλειτος, τέμνοντες
καίοντες πάντη βασανίζοντες κακῶς τοὺς
ἀρρωστοῦντας ἐπαιτιέονται μηδέν᾽ ἄξιον
μισθὸν λαμβάνειν παρὰ τῶν ἀρρωστοῦντων,
ταῦτα ἐργαζόμενοι τὰ ἀγαθὰ καὶ τὰς νόσους.

56

The cosmos works
by harmony of tensions,
like the lyre and bow.

*Cosmos adapts
to the tension
produced by the
object*

*harmonize is
an adjustment
of the instruments*

*fit, adapt, accommodate
"feedback loop"*

57

Therefore, good
and ill are one.

58

Good and ill to the physician
surely must be one,
since he derives his fee
from torturing the sick.

59

Συνάψιες οὖλα καὶ οὐχὶ οὖλα,
συμφερόμενον διαφερόμενον, συνᾷδον
διᾷδον· ἐκ πάντων ἓν καὶ ἐξ ἑνὸς πάντα.

60

Δίκης οὔνομα οὐκ ἂν ᾔδεσαν, εἰ ταῦτα μὴ
ἦν.

61

Ἡράκλειτος λέγει, ὡς τῷ μὲν θεῷ καλὰ
πάντα καὶ ἀγαθὰ καὶ δίκαια, ἄνθρωποι δὲ ἃ
μὲν ἄδικα ὑπειλήφασιν, ἃ δὲ δίκαια.

59

Two made one are never one.
Arguing the same we disagree.
Singing together we compete.
We choose each other
to be one, and from the one
both soon diverge.

60

Without injustices,
the name of justice
would mean what?

61

While cosmic wisdom
understands all things
are good and just,
intelligence may find
injustice here, and justice
somewhere else.

62

Εἰδέναι χρὴ τὸν πόλεμον ἐόντα ξυνόν, καὶ
δίκην ἔριν· καὶ γινόμενα πάντα κατ᾽ ἔριν καὶ
χρεώμενα.

63

Ἔστι γὰρ εἱμαρμένα πάντως . . .

64

Θάνατός ἐστι ὁκόσα ἐγερθέντες ὁρέομεν,
ὁκόσα δὲ εὕδοντες ὕπνος.

65

Ἓν τὸ σοφὸν μοῦνον λέγεσθαι οὐκ ἐθέλει
καὶ ἐθέλει Ζηνὸς οὔνομα.

62

Justice in our minds is strife.
We cannot help but see
war makes us as we are.

63

Thus are things decreed by fate.

64

Though what the waking see is deadly,
what the sleeping see is death.

65

The oneness of all wisdom
may be found, or not,
under the name of God.

66

Τοῦ βιοῦ οὔνομα βίος, ἔργον δὲ θάνατος.

67

Ἀθάνατοι θνητοί, θνητοί ἀθάνατοι, ζῶντες
τὸν ἐκείνων θάνατον τὸν δὲ ἐκείνων βίον
τεθνεῶτες.

68

Ψυχῇσι γὰρ θάνατος ὕδωρ γενέσθαι, ὕδατι
δὲ θάνατος γῆν γενέσθαι· ἐκ γῆς δὲ ὕδωρ
γίνεται, ἐξ ὕδατος δὲ ψυξή.

66

The living, when the dead
wood of the bow
springs back to life, must die.

67

Gods live past our meager death.
We die past their ceaseless living.

68

As souls change into water
on their way through death,
so water changes into earth.
And as water springs from earth,
so from water does the soul.

69

Ὁδὸς ἄνω κάτω μία καὶ ὡυτή.

70

Ξυνὸν ἀρχὴ καὶ πέρας.

71

Ψυχῆς πείρατα οὐκ ἂν ἐξεύροιο πᾶσαν
ἐπιπορευόμενος ὁδόν· οὕτω βαθὺν λόγον ἔχει.

69

The way up is the way back.

70

The beginning is the end.

71

The soul is undiscovered,
though explored forever
to a depth beyond report.

72

Ψυχῇσι τέρψις ὑγρῇσι γενέσθαι.

73

Ἀνὴρ ὁκότ' ἂν μεθυσθῇ, ἄγεται ὑπὸ παιδὸς
ἀνήβου σφαλλόμενος, οὐκ ἐπαΐων ὅκη βαίνει,
ὑγρὴν τὴν ψυχὴν ἔχων.

74

Αὔη ψυχὴ σοφωτάτη καὶ ἀρίστη.

72

Moisture makes the soul
succumb to joy.

73

An old drunk
leaning on a youngster,
saturated with bad wine,
head weaker than his feet . . .

74

Dry, the soul
grows wise
and good.

75

Αὐγὴ ξηρὴ ψυχὴ σοφοτάτη καὶ ἀρίστη.

76

Οὗ γῆ ξηρή, ψυχὴ σοφοτάτη καὶ ἀρίστη.

77

Ἄνθρωπος, ὅκως ἐν εὐφρόνῃ φάος,
ἅπτεται ἀποσβέννυται.

78

Ταὔτ᾽ εἶναι ζῶν καὶ τεθνηκός, καὶ τὸ
ἐγρηγορὸς καὶ τὸ καθεῦδον, καὶ νέον καὶ
γηραιόν· τάδε γὰρ μεταπεσόντα ἐκεῖνα ἐστι
κἀκεῖνα πάλιν μεταπεσόντα ταῦτα.

75

A dry light dries the earth.

76

See note.

77

A man in the quiet of the night
is kindled like a fire soon quenched.

p92 78 *B88*

Only the living may be dead,
the waking sleep,   *rebuke to Hesod*
the young be old.   *for failing to observe*
                        the unity of day
                        and night.

79

Αἰὼν παῖς ἐστι παίζων πεσσεύων· παιδὸς
ἡ βασιληίη.

80

Ἐδιζησάμην ἐμεωυτόν.

81

Ποταμοῖσι τοῖσι αὐτοῖσι ἐμβαίνομέν τε
καὶ οὐκ ἐμβαίνομεν, εἶμέν τε καὶ οὐκ εἶμεν.

79

Time is a game
played beautifully
by children.

80

Applicants for wisdom
do what I have done:
inquire within.

81

Just as the river where I step
is not the same, and is,
so I am as I am not.

82

Κάματός ἐστι τοῖς αὐτοῖς μοχθεῖν καὶ ἄρχεσθαι.

83

Μεταβάλλον ἀναπαύεται.

84

Καὶ ὁ κυκεὼν διίσταται μὴ κινεόμενος.

85

Νέκυες κοπρίων ἐκβλητότεροι.

82

The rule that makes
its subject weary
is a sentence
of hard labor.

83

For this reason,
change gives rest.

84

Goat cheese melted
in warm wine congeals
if not well stirred.

85

Corpses, like night soil,
get carted off.

86

Γενόμενοι ζώειν ἐθέλουσι μόρους τ' ἔχειν·
μᾶλλον δὲ ἀναπαύεσθαι, καὶ παῖδας
καταλείπουσι μόρους γενέσθαι.

87

Οἱ μὲν "ἡβῶντος" ἀναγινώσκοντες ἔτη
τριάκοντα ποιοῦσι τὴν γενέαν καθ'
Ἑράκλειτον· ἐν ᾧ χρόνῳ γεννῶντα παρέχει τὸν
ἐξ αὑτοῦ γεγεννημένον ὁ γεννήσας.

88

Ὅθεν οὐκ ἀπὸ σκοποῦ Ἡράκλειτος
γενεὰν τὸν μῆνα καλεῖ.

86

The living, though they yearn
for consummation of their fate,
need rest, and in their turn leave
children to fulfill their doom.

87

In thirty years a newborn boy
can grow to father him a son
who grows by then
to father sons himself.

88

Thirty, therefore, names
the moon of generation.

89

Ex homine in tricennio potest avus haberi.

90

'Εργάτας εἶναι λέγει καὶ συνεργοὺς τῶν ἐν
τῷ κόσμῳ γινομένων.

89

Look: the baby born
under the new moon
under the old moon holds
her grandchild in her arms.

90

Even a soul submerged in sleep
is hard at work, and helps
make something of the world.

Ξυνόν ἐστι πᾶσι τὸ φρονέειν. ξὺν νόῳ
λέγοντας ἰσχυρίζεσθαι χρὴ τῷ ξυνῷ πάντων,
ὅκωσπερ νόμῳ πόλις καὶ πολὺ ἰσχυροτέρως.
τρέφονται γὰρ πάντες οἱ ἀνθρώπειοι νόμοι ὑπὸ
ἑνὸς τοῦ θείου· κρατέει γὰρ τοσοῦτον ὁκόσον
ἐθέλει καὶ ἐξαρκέει πᾶσι καὶ περιγίνεται.

91

Since mindfulness, of all things,
is the ground of being,
to speak one's true mind,
and to keep things known
in common, serves all being,
just as laws made clear
uphold the city,
yet with greater strength.
Of all pronouncements of the law
the one source is the Word
whereby we choose what helps
true mindfulness prevail.

92

Διὸ δεῖ ἕπεσθαι τῷ ξυνῷ. τοῦ λόγου δ᾽
ἐόντος ξυνοῦ, ζώουσι οἱ πολλοὶ ὡς ἰδίην
ἔχοντες φρόνησιν.

93

Ὧι μάλιστα διηνεκέως ὁμιλέουσι, τούτῳ
διαφέρονται.

92

Although we need the Word
to keep things known in common,
people still treat specialists
as if their nonsense
were a form of wisdom.

93

Fools seek counsel
from the ones they doubt.

94

Οὐ δεῖ ὥσπερ καθεύδοντας ποιεῖν καὶ
λέγειν.

95

Τοῖς ἐγρηγορόσιν ἕνα καὶ κοινὸν κόσμον
εἶναι, τῶν δὲ κοιμωμένων ἕκαστον εἰς ἴδιον
ἀποστρέφεσθαι.

96

Ἦθος γὰρ ἀνθρώπειον μὲν οὐκ ἔχει
γνώμας, θεῖον δὲ ἔχει.

97

Ἀνὴρ νήπιος ἤκουσε πρὸς δαίμονος
ὄκωσπερ παῖς πρὸς ἀνδρός.

94

People need not act and speak
as if they were asleep.

95

The waking have one world
in common. Sleepers
meanwhile turn aside, each
into a darkness of his own.

96

The habit of knowledge
is not human but divine.

97

The language of a grown man,
to the cosmic powers,
sounds like babytalk to men.

98

’Ανθρώπων ὁ σοφώτατος πρὸς θεὸν πίθηκος
φανεῖται καὶ σοφίᾳ καὶ κάλλει καὶ τοῖς
ἄλλοις πᾶσιν.

99

Πιθήκων ὁ κάλλιστος αἰσχρὸς ἄλλῳ γένει
συμβάλλειν.

98

To a god the wisdom
of the wisest man
sounds apish. Beauty
in a human face
looks apish too.
In everything
we have attained
the excellence of apes.

99

 The ape apes find
most beautiful
looks apish
to non-apes.

100

Μάχεσθαι χρὴ τὸν δῆμον ὑπὲρ τοῦ νόμου
ὅκως ὑπὲρ τείχεος.

101

Μόροι γὰρ μέζονες μέζονας μοίρας
λαγχάνουσι.

102

Ἀρηιφάτους θεοὶ τιμῶσι καὶ ἄνθρωποι.

103

Ὕβριν χρή σβεννύειν μᾶλλον ἢ πυρκαϊήν.

100

People ought to fight
to keep their law
as to defend the city's walls.

101

 The luckiest men die
worthwhile deaths.

102

Gods, like men, revere the boys
who die for them in battle.

103

Insolence needs drowning
worse than wildfire.

104

’Ανθρώποισι γίνεσθαι ὁκόσα θέλουσι οὐκ
ἄμεινον. νοῦσος ὑγίειαν ἐποίησε ἡδύ, κακὸν
ἀγαθόν, λιμὸς κόρον, κάματος ἀνάπαυσιν.

105

Θυμῷ μάχεσθαι χαλεπόν· ὅ τι γὰρ ἂν χρηίζῃ
γίνεσθαι, ψυχῆς ὠνέεται.

104

Always having what we want
may not be the best good fortune.
Health seems sweetest
after sickness, food
in hunger, goodness
in the wake of evil, and at the end
of daylong labor sleep.

105

Yearning hurts,
and what release
may come of it
feels much like death.

106

Ἀνθρώποισι πᾶσι μέτεστι γιγνώσκειν ἑαυτοὺς
καὶ σωφρονεῖν.

107

Σωφρονεῖν ἀρετὴ μεγίστη· καὶ σοφίη ἀληθέα
λέγειν καὶ ποιεῖν κατὰ φύσιν ἐπαΐοντας.

106

All people ought to know themselves
and everyone be wholly mindful.

107

To be evenminded
is the greatest virtue.
Wisdom is to speak
the truth and act
in keeping with its nature.

108

Ἀμαθίη ἄμεινον κρύπτειν· ἔργον δὲ ἐν ἀνέσει
καὶ παρ' οἶνον.

109

Κρύπτειν ἀμαθίην κρέσσον ἢ ἐς τὸ μέσον
φέρειν.

110

Νόμος καὶ βουλῇ πείθεσθαι ἑνός.

108

Not to be quite such a fool
sounds good. The trick,
with so much wine
and easy company, is how.

109

Stupidity is better
kept a secret
than displayed.

110

Sound thinking
is to listen well and choose
one course of action.

Τίς γὰρ αὐτῶν νόος ἢ φρήν ; [δήμων] ἀοιδοῖσι
ἕπονται καὶ διδασκάλῳ χρέωνται ὁμίλῳ, οὐκ
εἰδότες ὅτι πολλοὶ κακοὶ ὀλίγοι δὲ ἀγαθοι.
αἱρεῦνται γὰρ ἓν ἀντία πάντων οἱ ἄριστοι,
κλέος ἀέναον θνητῶν, οἱ δὲ πολλοὶ κεκόρηνται
ὅκωσπερ κτήνεα.

111

What use are these people's wits,
who let themselves be led
by speechmakers, in crowds,
without considering
how many fools and thieves
they are among, and how few
choose the good?
The best choose progress
toward one thing, a name
forever honored by the gods,
while others eat their way
toward sleep like nameless oxen.

112

’Εν Πριήνῃ Βίας ἐγένετο ὁ Τευτάμεω, οὗ
πλέων λόγος ἢ τῶν ἄλλων.

113

Εἷς ἐμοὶ μύριοι, ἐὰν ἄριστος ᾖ.

112

Not far from the ancient city
of Miletus lived
the son of Teutamas,
whose name was Bias.
I would have it known,
this one man more than others
earned the good esteem
of worthy people.

113

Give me one man
from among ten thousand,
if he be the best.

"Αξιον Ἐφεσίοις ἡβηδὸν ἀπάγξασθαι πᾶσι καὶ
τοῖς ἀνήβοις τὴν πόλιν καταλιπεῖν, οἵτινες
Ἑρμόδωρον ἄνδρα ἑωυτῶν ὀνήιστον
ἐξέβαλον, φάντες· ἡμέων μηδὲ εἷς ὀνήιστος
ἔστω, εἰ δὲ μή, ἄλλῃ τε καὶ μετ' ἄλλων.

114

As for the Ephesians,
I would have them, youths,
elders, and all those between,
go hang themselves, leaving the city
in the abler hands of children.
With banishment of Hermodoros
they say, No man should be
worthier than average. Thus,
my fellow citizens declare,
whoever would seek
excellence can find it
elsewhere among others.

115

Κύνες καὶ βαΰζουσι ὃν ἂν μὴ γινώσκωσι.

116

Ἀπιστίη διαφυγγάνει μὴ γινώσκεσθαι.

117

Βλὰξ ἄνθρωπος ἐπὶ παντὶ λόγῳ ἐπτοῆσθαι
φιλέει.

118

Δοκεόντα ὁ δοκιμώτατος γινώσκει φυλάσσειν·
καὶ μέντοι καὶ δίκη καταλήψεται ψευδέων
τέκτονας καὶ μάρτυρας.

115

Dogs, by this same logic, bark
at what they cannot understand.

116

What is not yet known
those blinded by bad faith
can never learn.

117

Stupidity is doomed,
therefore, to cringe
at every syllable
of wisdom.

118

While those who mouth high talk
may think themselves high-minded,
justice keeps the book
on hypocrites and liars.

119

Τόν θ' Ὅμηρον ἔφασκεν ἄξιον ἐκ τῶν ἀγώνων
ἐκβάλλεσθαι καὶ ῥαπίζεσθαι, καὶ Ἀρχίλοχον
ὁμοίως.

120

Unus dies par omni est.

121

Ἦθος ἀνθρώπῳ δαίμων.

122

Ἀνθρώπους μένει τελευτήσαντας ἄσσα οὐκ
ἔλπονται οὐδὲ δοκέουσι.

119

Homer I deem worthy—
in a trial by combat—
of good cudgeling,
and Archilochos the same.

120

Any day stands
equal to the rest.

121

One's bearing
shapes one's fate.

122

After death comes
nothing hoped for
nor imagined.

123

Ἐπανίστασθαι καὶ φύλακας γίνεσθαι ἐγερτὶ
ζώντων καὶ νεκρῶν.

124

Νυκτιπόλοι, μάγοι, βάκχοι, λῆναι, μύσται.

123

The revenant keeps watch
over the dead and living.

124

Nightwalker, magus,
and their entourage,
bacchants and mystics
of the wine press,
with stained faces
and damp wits . . .

125

Τὰ γὰρ νομιζόμενα κατ᾽ ἀνθρώπους μυστήρια
ἀνιερωστὶ μυεῦνται.

126

Καὶ τοῖς ἀγάλμασι τουτέοισι εὔχονται, ὁκοῖον
εἴ τις τοῖς δόμοισι λεσχηνεύοιτο, οὔ τι γινώσκων
θεοὺς οὐδ᾽ ἥρωας, οἵτινες εἰσι.

125

Initiation, here,
into the ancient mysteries
so honored among men
mocks holiness.

126

They raise their voices
at stone idols
as a man might argue
with his doorpost,
they have understood
so little of the gods.

Εἰ μὴ γὰρ Διονύσῳ πομπὴν ἐποιεῦντο καὶ
ὕμνεον ᾆσμα αἰδοίοισι, ἀναιδέστατα εἴργαστ'
ἄν· ὡυτὸς δὲ Ἀΐδης καὶ Διόνυσος, ὅτεῳ
μαίνονται καὶ ληναΐζουσι.

127

Dionysus is their name for death.
And if they did not claim
the statue of the drunk

they worshipped was a god,
or call their incoherent song
about his cock their hymn,
everyone would know
what filth their shamelessness
has made of them
and of the name of god.

128

Θυσιῶν τοίνυν τίθημι διττὰ εἴδη· τὰ μὲν τῶν
ἀποκεκαθαρμένων παντάπασιν ἀνθρώπων, οἷα
ἐφ' ἑνὸς' ἄν ποτε γένοιτο σπανίως, ὥς φησιν
Ἡράκλειτος, ἤ τινων ὀλίγων εὐαριθμήτων
ἀνδρῶν· τὰ δ' ἔνυλα καὶ σωματοειδῆ καὶ διὰ
μεταβολῆς συνιστάμενα, οἷα τοῖς ἔτι
κατεχομένοις ὑπὸ τοῦ σώματος ἁρμόζει.

129

Καθαίρονται δὲ αἵματι μιαινόμενοι ὥσπερ ἂν
εἴ τις ἐς πηλὸν ἐμβὰς πηλῷ ἀπονίζοιτο.

130

Ἄκεα.

128

A sacred ritual
may be performed by one
entirely purified but seldom.
Other rites belong to those
confined in the sodden
lumber of the body.

129

Tainted souls who try
to purify themselves with blood
are like the man
who steps in filth and thinks
to bathe in sewage.

130

Silence, healing.

Notes

On the order: This book retains, in all but a few places, the ordering and numbering of fragments from Bywater's nineteenth-century arrangement, grouped by topic. My deviations from Bywater are noted below. In the early twentieth century, Diels believed that an alphabetical arrangement of the fragments, because it was random, was less tendentious. Wheelwright, on the other hand, observes that Diels himself has been tendentious in using the discontinuity of his arrangement to show that the writings of Heraclitus were not a coherent whole. In my translation, the ordering of fragments, word choice, transitional logic, emphasis on threads of meaning, and so on serve my own best inklings of a coherence and lucidity that have survived the destruction and imperfect representation of what Heraclitus wrote.

1. Bywater 1 and 2 are transposed here to put the poetic passage about the Word first, as several translators have already done. The usual translation of the Greek *logos* has been "Word." This reverberates with the diction in the Standard Version of the Gospel Ac-

cording to John: "In the beginning was the Word."
John must have had the powerful tradition of Hera-
clitean thought in mind when he used this term in
his original Greek. *Logos* indicates not only the lexical
word, but also all means of making ideas known, as
well as ideas themselves, the phenomena to which
ideas respond, and the rules that govern both phe-
nomena and ideas. The holistic logic *(logos)* of this
range of meanings must have been a large part of the
word's appeal, as the next fragment confirms. In the
second sentence in the Greek, ambiguous syntax
may suggest that Heraclitus separated the essences of
things and said how each thing truly is. It may mean,
on the other hand, that the ignorant fail to do this.
The latter seems more plausible, since Heraclitus
makes no other such personal claim for his accom-
plishment, but insists repeatedly on the limits of
such claims, as in the next fragment.

2. See the note on 1.

9. The discussion of Heraclitus here omitted is
from the *Suda,* or *Suidas,* an unreliable literary ency-
clopedia from about the tenth century C.E.

11. See the note on 12.

12. The Greek word *Sibylla,* or "Sibyl," appears in
this fragment for the first time ever. No one knows
where it came from. *Ton theon,* "the god" of sibylline
prophecy, *Ho anax* of the previous fragment, was the
Lord Apollo, god of prophetic wisdom and of the

cosmic fire of the sun. For more about the word *theos,* see the Introduction.

16. I have provided my own examples from Hesiod and Pythagoras in this and the next fragment, to illustrate their supposed folly. Heraclitus, no doubt, would have chosen other examples.

17. See note on 16.

24. The usual translation of *koros,* as satiety, gives the literal meaning, but loses the strong connotation of insolence, important to the personifying logic of this and many other fragments.

31. Jones's literal translation of this fragment is: "If there were no sun, there would be night, in spite of the other stars." Because the sense of the Greek seems incomplete, I introduce the questions into my translation, to suggest possible connections with the logic of reversal in fragments 35, 36, and elsewhere.

35. This rough paraphrase introduces the mention of gods and monsters to clarify the distinction between the polymorphous concreteness of Hesiod and the unifying abstract thought Heraclitus preferred.

36. The exact phrasing of the original Greek is difficult, but scholars agree about the general sense. I have simplified the second half, which says literally that fire mixed with various spices assumes various names.

41. This, the most famous fragment, is usually

translated: "You cannot step in the same river twice."
According to Plutarch, Heraclitus says, "You cannot
step into the same rivers twice." My rephrasing tries
to clear away distractingly familiar language from a
startling thought. It seems unlikely to my mind that
the ancient authors who refer to this idea quote Her-
aclitus exactly.

42. Here Stobaeus quotes Arius Didymus's report
of what Cleanthes thought about what Heraclitus
said. I have omitted this as a less interesting and less
reliable version of the same passage as reported by
Plutarch in fragment 41.

51. Heraclitus is quoted as saying, "An ass prefers
straw [or refuse] to gold." Aristotle, who takes this to
refer to food, does not say whether the reference to
food is explicit in the original or his own inference.

53. This fragment, like fragments 89 and 120, ex-
ists only in a Latin paraphrase of the Greek.

54. This fragment is omitted as repetition of the
second part of 53.

60. I have introduced a question here to compen-
sate for a vagueness that seems to come from loss of
context.

66. An untranslatable pun in this fragment in-
volves the Greek words for bow and life, *biós* and
bíos.

76. Fragments 74, 75, and 76 overlap. This trans-
lation separates the sense of 74 and 75, and omits 76.

89. This fragment, like fragments 53 and 120, exists only in a Latin paraphrase of the Greek.

112. The name of the town here is Phriene. But little is known about Phriene, so I mention nearby Miletus instead. Miletus was an important city from the heyday of Minoan culture until the Ionian revolt in Heraclitus's time.

120. This fragment, like fragments 53 and 89, exists only in a Latin paraphrase of the Greek.

121. This fragment is often translated: "Character is fate." More literally, a man's *ethos* is his *daimon*. A person's customary ways of being and acting, in other words, are that person's guiding genius. I prefer the crisper phrasing, "Character is fate," because the Greek is crisp, but meanings lost in the pithier version seem worth keeping.

129. Fragments 129 and 130 are transposed for the sake of resolution.

130. The one word, *akê*, has several meanings: silence, calm, lulling, healing.

Bibliography

The following books contain translations into English or commentary in English or both.

Burnet, John. *Early Greek Philosophy* (London, 1892).

Davenport, Guy. *Herakelitos and Diogenes* (Bolinas, 1979).

Jones, H. W. S. "Heraclitus on the Universe," in Volume IV of the Works of Hippocrates (Loeb Classical Library, 1931).

Kahn, Charles H. *Art and Thought of Heraclitus* (Cambridge, 1979).

Kirk, G. S. *Heraclitus, the Cosmic Fragments* (Cambridge, 1954).

Wheelwright, Philip. *Heraclitus* (Princeton, 1959).